BULLDOG COLORING BOOK

Directed by:

Angela Wesbey

illustrated by:

Jason Wesbey

Welcome to the family. Some of the following images are simple and some may be complicated; you can decide which ones are fun. Thanks for taking this journey with us.

I0171160

EMPTY.

EMPTY

STILL NOTHING.....

SURPRISE!

STILL NOTHING.....

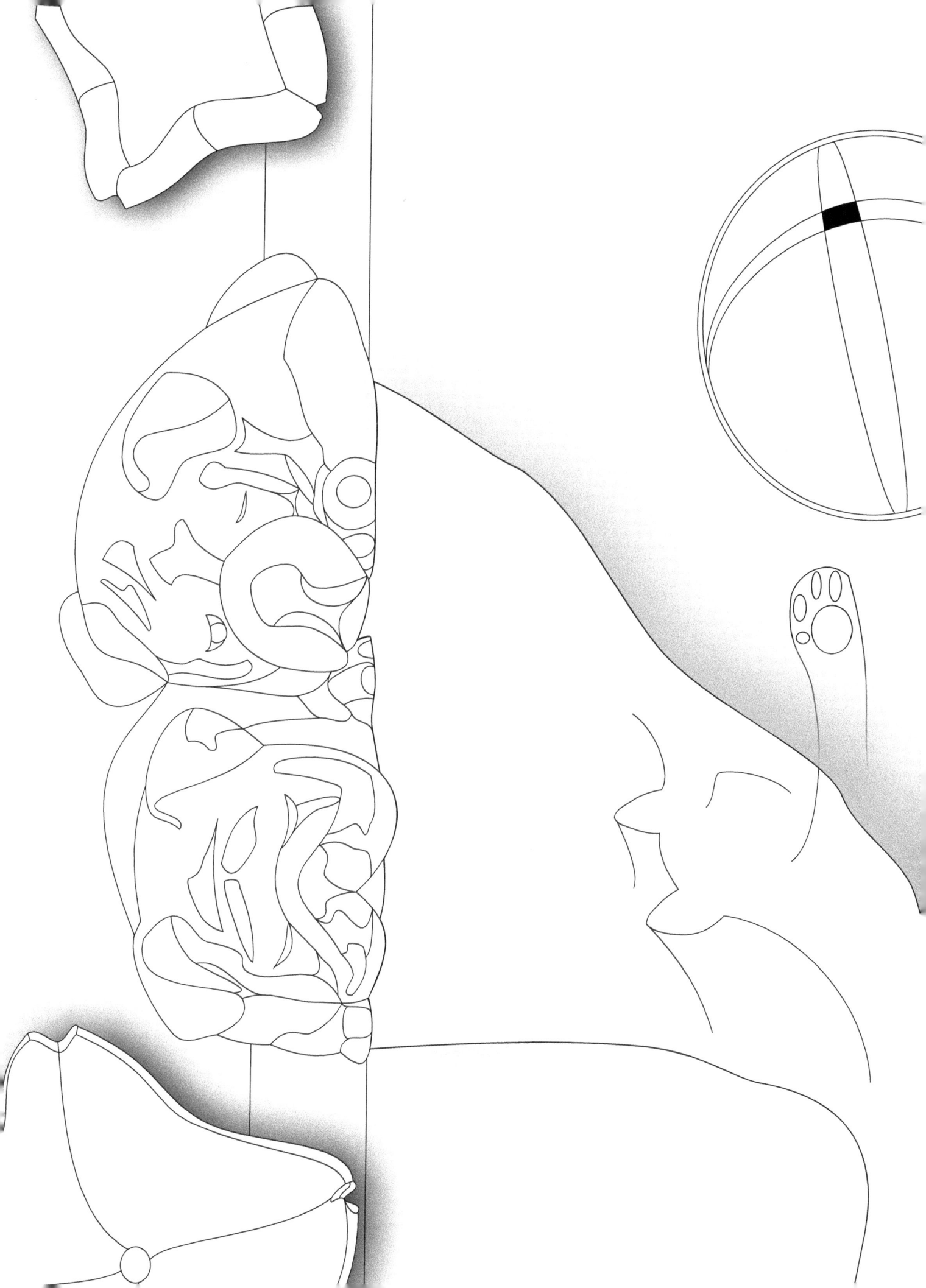

HA, GOTCHA...

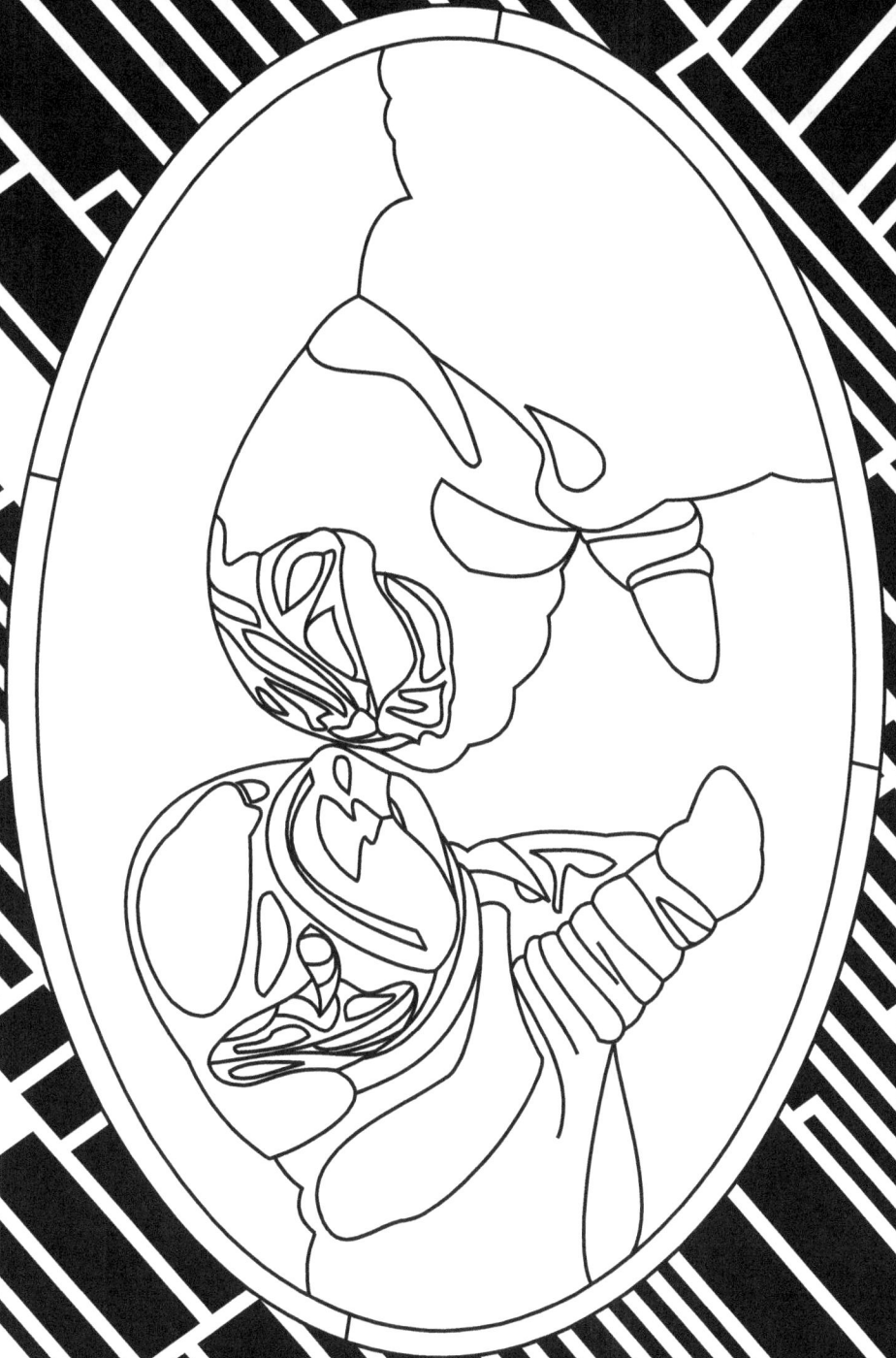

NOW, I'M JUST MAD.........

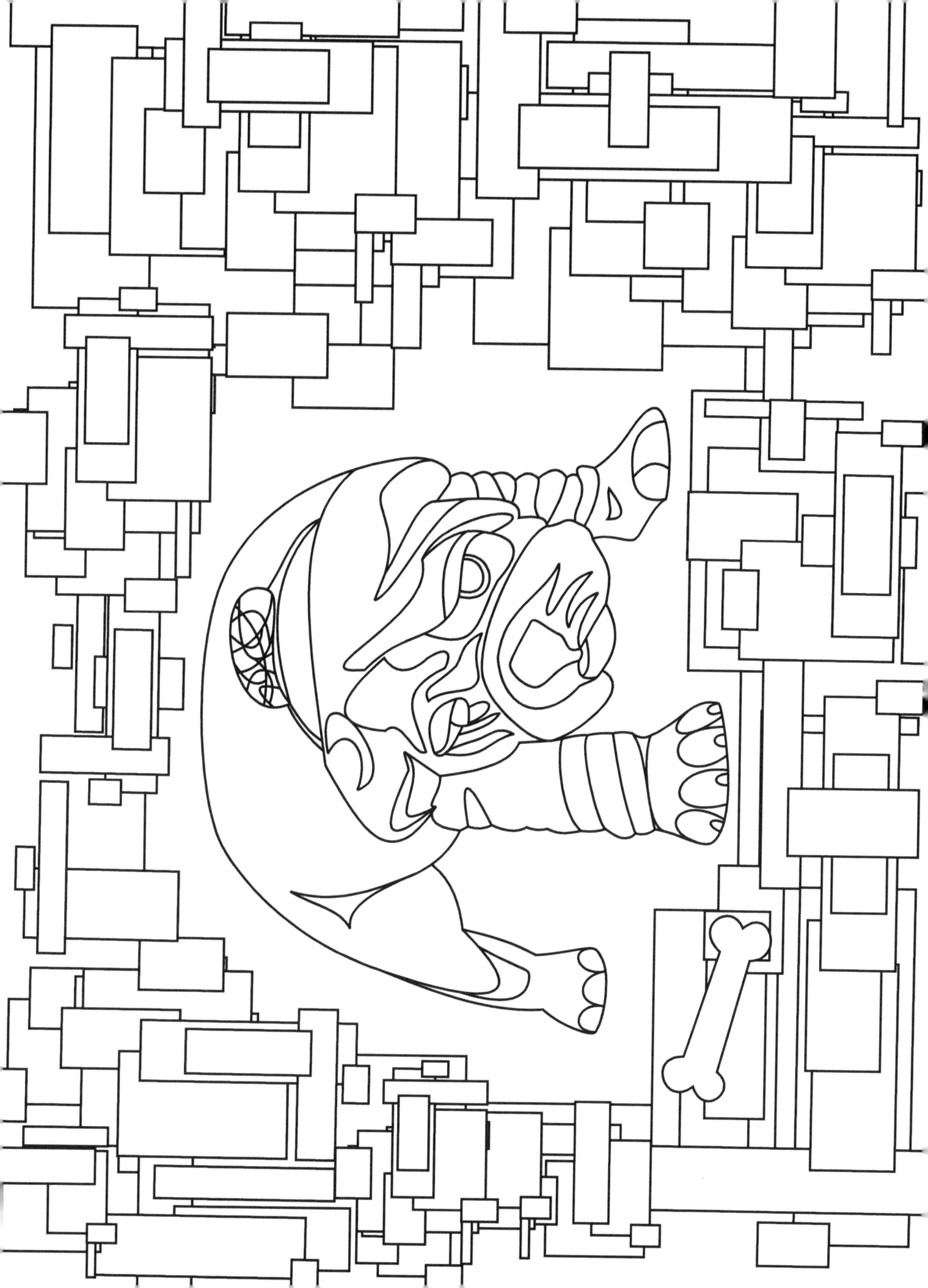

REALLY?

STOP LOOKING

KNOCK, KNOCK?

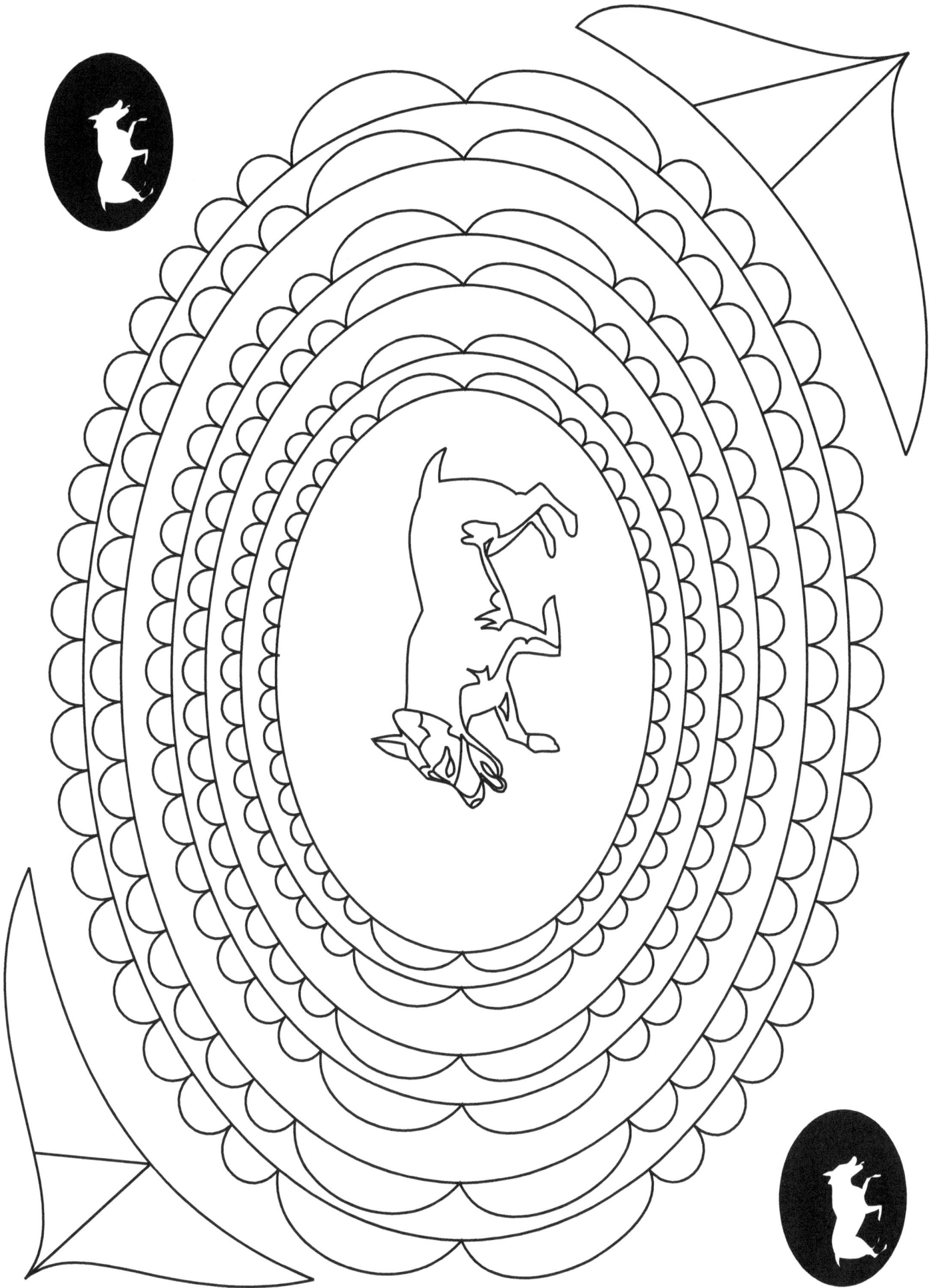

BULLDOG

IF YOU SAID, "BULLDOG WHO?" I'LL PLAY ALONG ON THE NEXT PAGE. REMEMBER, YOU ASKED.

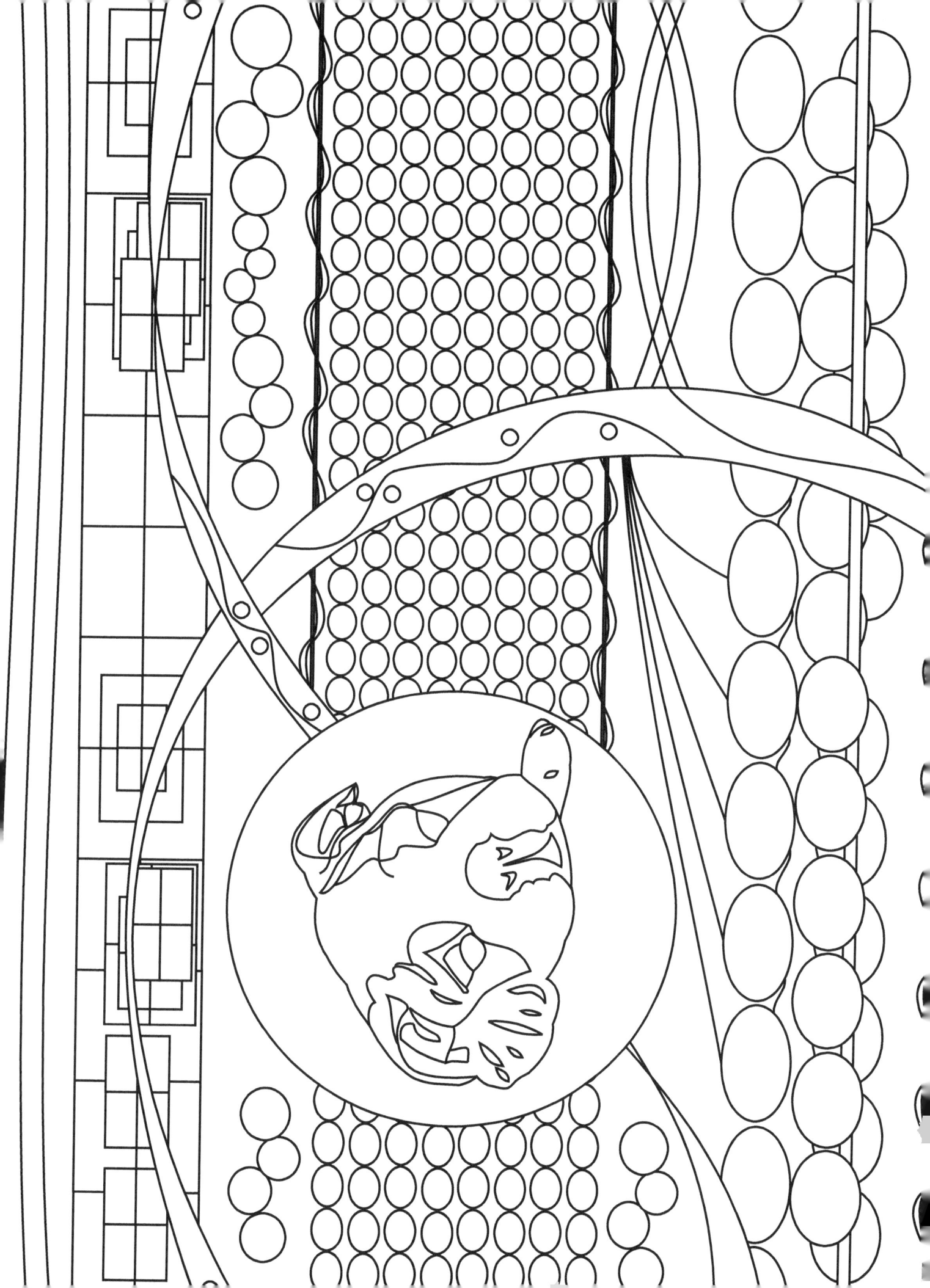

BULLDOG WHO ....

EMPTY.

EMPTY

EMPTY

EMPTY

EMPTY

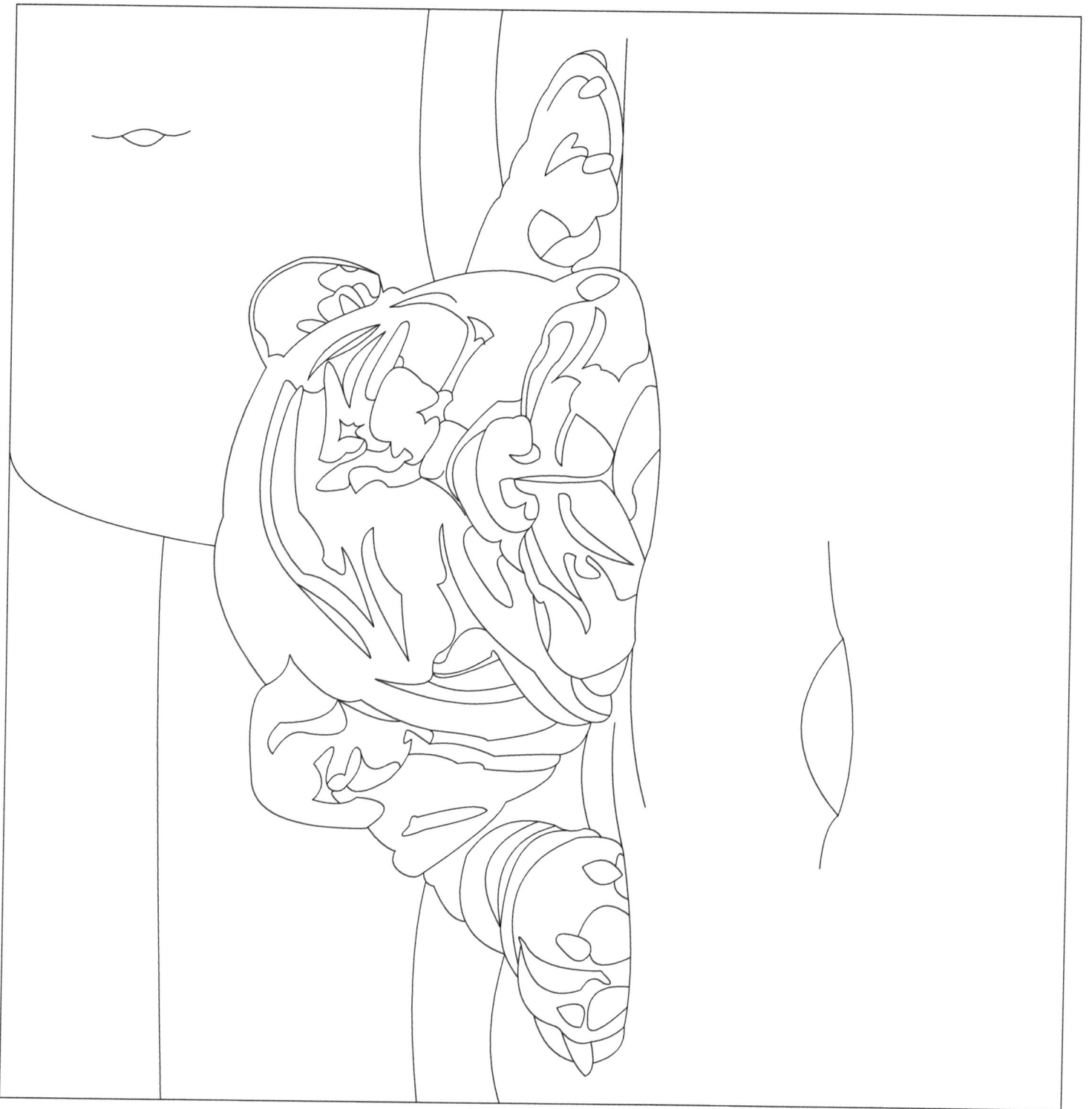

EMPTY.

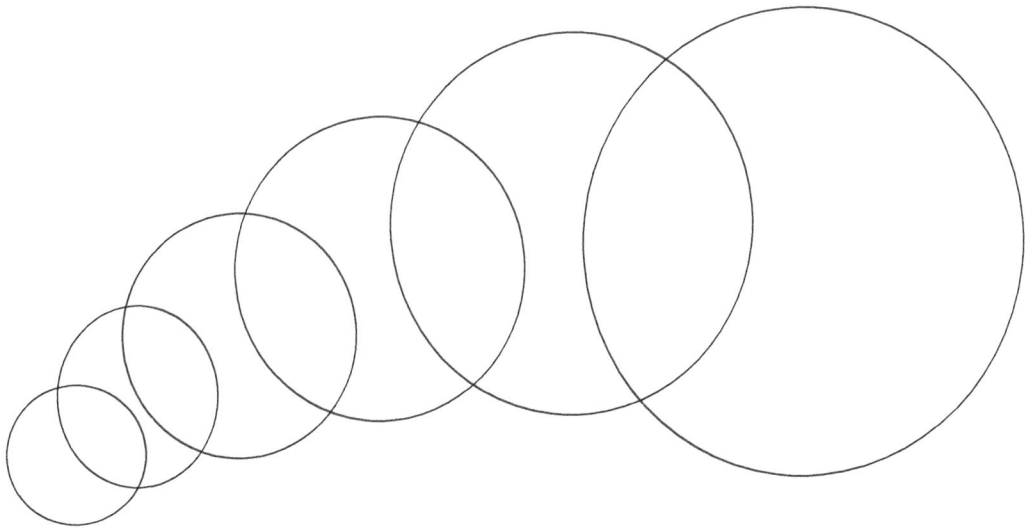

EMPTY

EMPTY.

Can you draw a bulldog? Here's your chance to shine.....

Speaking of shining...

The better photos found in this book were

provided by: **Kim Henry Photography**

Special thanks to:

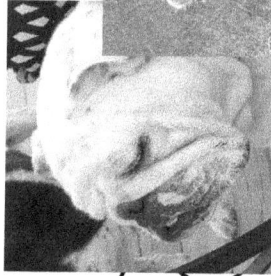

Playing in yard

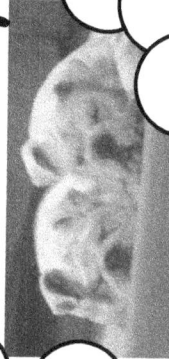

Sawyer

while Sawyer is interested in the cat

Dojo

Sleeping standing up

Dojo sleeps laying down

Frank

Who doesn't have a pet spider?

Miss B

Grand Champion and she knows it...

Apache
Still cute

only had her a few days

Miya

Now, enjoying retirement

Jitter

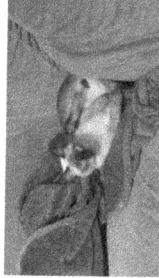

Speak for themselves

Dip

Guest appearances by:

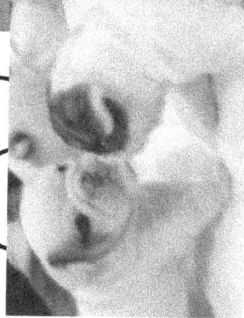

Play time

Storm
Super smart, dumb dog...

www.ingramcontent.com/pod-product-compliance
Lightning Source LLC
Chambersburg PA
CBHW080553030426

42337CB00024B/4855